eco GUIDES

A Teen Guide to

Eco-Leisure

Neil Morris

Raintree

Raintree is an imprint of Capstone Global Library Limited, a company incorporated in England and Wales having its registered office at 7 Pilgrim Street, London, EC4V 6LB – Registered company number: 6695582

To contact Raintree:
Phone: 0845 6044371
Fax: + 44 (0) 1865 312263
Email: myorders@raintreepublishers.co.uk
Outside the UK please telephone +44 1865 312262.

Edited by Andrew Farrow, Adam Miller, and Vaarunika Dharmapala
Designed by Richard Parker
Original illustrations © Capstone Global Library Ltd 2013
Illustrated by HL Studios
Picture research by Tracy Cummins
Originated by Capstone Global Library Ltd
Printed and bound in China by CTPS

ISBN 978 1 406 24986 6
16 15 14 13 12
10 9 8 7 6 5 4 3 2 1

British Library Cataloguing in Publication Data
Morris, Neil.
A teen guide to eco-leisure. -- (Eco guides)
790.1-dc23
A full catalogue record for this book is available from the British Library.

Acknowledgements
We would like to thank the following for permission to reproduce photographs: Alamy p. 8 (© Gavin Hellier); Capstone Library p. 20 (Karon Dubke); Corbis p. 5 (© Tom Bol/Aurora Photos), 10 (© Darren Kemper), 14 (© Tomas Rodriguez), 22 (© David Burton/Beateworks), 26 (© Mika), 32 (© Atlantide Phototravel); Getty Images pp. 7 (Fabrice Dimier/Bloomberg), 13 (TORSTEN BLACKWOOD/AFP), 23 (Mike Harrington), 28 (Blend Images/Moxie Productions), 35 (Lee Strickland), 36 (Andersen Ross), 45 (Laurence Monneret), 46 (altrendo images); istockphoto pp. 42 (© iztok noc), 49 (© Jennifer Byron); Newscom pp. 31 (TELAM Xinhua News Agency), 40 (David Barnes/ DanitaDelimont.com "Danita Delimont Photography"); Shutterstock pp. 4 (Ryan Rodrick Beiler), 9 (Undergroundarts.co.uk), 12 (Volodymyr Goinyk), 15 (Perry Harmon), 16 (Lana K), 17 (John Kasawa), 18 (Darko Zeljkovic), 19 (Lowe Llaguno), 25 (Anatoliy Samara), 27 (Roman Sotola), 29 (rehoboth foto), 30 (Hallgerd), 34 (Ipatov), 37, 39 (l i g h t p o e t), 43 (JustASC); Superstock p. 33 (© Jim West/ age footstock).

Cover photograph of young couple in woodland reproduced with permission of Corbis (© Juice Images). Cover logo reproduced with permission of Shutterstock (Olivier Le Moal).

Contents

Why be green? 4

Green options at home 14

Fun with friends 24

Travelling green 36

Eco-holidays 42

Summing up: it's your choice! 48

Quiz 50

Glossary 52

Find out more 54

Index 56

Some words are shown in bold, **like this**. You can find out what they mean by looking in the glossary.

Important!
Please check with an adult before doing the projects in this book.

Why be green?

Leisure is important to all of us. It is the free time we use to enjoy ourselves. What about eco-leisure? Well, "eco" is short for ecology – the scientific study of how organisms relate to each other and to their surroundings. So, "eco-leisure" means doing things in your spare time that are helpful to the environment. This could mean recycling junk, saving energy, or getting involved in local projects. You can do all these things and still enjoy your free time. In fact, being green can help you get even more pleasure from your leisure!

So, what does green mean?

Since the early 1970s, the word "green" has been used to mean *environmental* or *environmentally friendly*. This use of the word originally came from the colour's links with grass and plants. If you go green, you try to live your life in a way that does as little harm as possible to the environment. This includes all Earth's land and sea, as well as the air that we breathe.

In 1971, a small group of environmentalists started an organization called Greenpeace. It has become an influential, international movement. Today, many people around the world call for action on **climate change**.

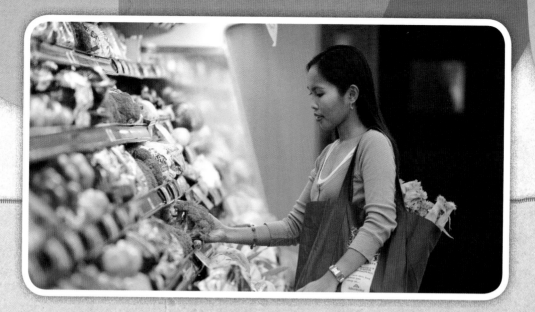

Plastic versus paper bags

- Paper is from a **renewable** source – managed forests. Plastic is from non-renewable oil.
- It takes nearly four times more energy and twenty times more water to manufacture a paper bag than to make a plastic one.
- Manufacturing paper and plastic causes acid rain and water pollution.
- It takes 91 per cent less energy to recycle a kilogram of plastic than a kilogram of paper. But people recycle more paper than plastic.
- Both are bad news in **landfill** sites, because they are slow to **degrade** and give off methane.

So, which is greener? Well, in a word ... neither! Reusable bags are best, such as those made from canvas.

Making a start

Don't let difficult eco-decisions put you off. The best way to start going green is by taking one step at a time. For example, you could keep on reusing plastic and paper bags until they are falling apart. Then you could put them in the recycling bin and get yourself a reusable bag.

Setting goals

A way to get started on being green in your leisure is to set yourself some goals and not try to do too much at once. You could look through this book and list some ideas you want to follow. Tick off the list items as you put them into action.

Why should I care?

Human life is dependent on the planet on which we live. We need its air to breathe, its water to drink, and its plants to eat. So, it makes sense to look after Earth. If we ruin it, we'll all suffer the consequences. We must also think of future generations.

But what's in it for me?

There are lots of personal advantages to being green. One is that you can save money. Think about two aspects of green living. The first is goods. Do you really need a new mobile phone or a new gadget? Resisting the latest trends can save you money, and damage the world around you less. You could ask yourself questions, as on the flowchart below. You might want a gizmo, but do you really need it? If so, and you think you can afford it, you could check this by doing the sums. How long do you think the new gizmo will last? How much will it cost per month? Are you sure it's better than the old one or worth it at all?

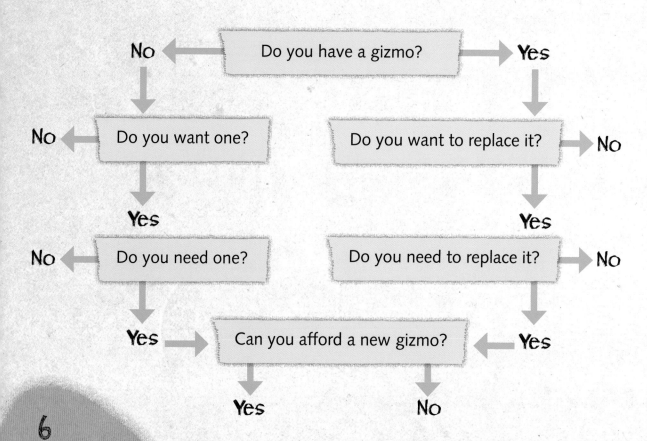

Saving energy and money

Then there's energy use. If you save on heating by putting on an extra sweater, or on electricity by switching things off, the bill-payer will face a much smaller charge. Admittedly, this might mean more to your parents than it does to you, but your family will save money. When you are older and pay the bills yourself, you will be used to saving energy and money.

Why me? What about others?

It won't just be your family who value your green contribution. Teachers and employers see awareness of green issues as an important aspect of everyone's education. So, your green experience could help you get the sort of career you want. It might also matter to your friends who would much rather hang out with a thoughtful person than a thoughtless one. You won't be alone, and you might find that there are local green groups or projects to join.

Companies bring out new models of their products, such as this iPad, all the time. The latest gadgets can be hard to resist, but do you really need them?

Combating climate change

Global warming and the resulting climate change are the most serious environmental problems facing the world today. Our planet's average global temperature has changed over millions of years, but in the 20th and early 21st centuries human activities have caused rising temperatures. They have added to the "greenhouse effect", which stops heat escaping from Earth in a similar way to glass trapping warmth inside a greenhouse.

Certain gases in the atmosphere, such as carbon dioxide (CO_2) and methane, cause the effect. We have been adding to these by emitting them from power plants, factories, and cars.

What's a carbon footprint?

We all have our own **carbon footprint**, which means the amount of carbon dioxide (CO_2) each of us produces in our daily lives. Most of this carbon **emission** comes through burning **fossil fuels** (coal, gas, and oil). In more economically developed parts of the world, energy use at home makes up about 27 per cent of each person's carbon footprint. Private transport makes up 10 per cent and public transport 3 per cent. Leisure accounts for 14 per cent of our total footprint. This includes emissions caused through the manufacture, delivery, and disposal of products and services we buy.

Eco Impact

This table shows the average person's carbon footprint in different countries. The figure is in tonnes of CO_2 per year.

Australia	18.9
Belize	1.4
Canada	16.4
China	5.3
Germany	9.6
India	1.5
Japan	9.5
Mali	0.1
Qatar	53.5
Russia	12.1
South Africa	8.8
United Kingdom	8.5
United States	17.5

By the way, a tonne of CO_2 gas is enough to fill nearly 34,000 party balloons.

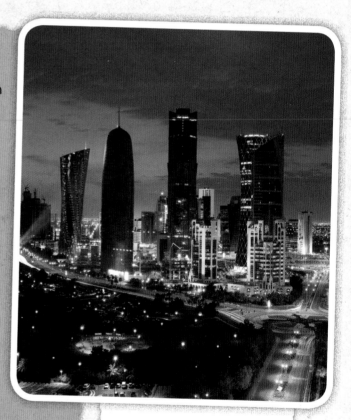

The 1.9 million people of Qatar, in the Middle East, have the world's biggest average carbon footprint. They use enormous amounts of electricity, especially on air conditioning. This is the night skyline of Qatar's capital Doha.

So, how big is *your* carbon footprint?

You can find carbon calculators on the internet:

- United Kingdom: carboncalculator.direct.gov.uk
- Australia: carbonneutral.com.au/carbon-calculator.html

The calculator will ask you questions about your home, your appliances, and your travel. At the end of the questionnaire, you will get your result and be able to compare it with others. The website will also give tips on how you can reduce your footprint.

Which of the following do you currently recycle at home?

NEWSPAPERS?	☐ YES	☐ NO
MAGAZINES?	☐ YES	☐ NO
GLASS?	☐ YES	☐ NO
ALUMINIUM AND STEEL CANS?	☐ YES	☐ NO
PLASTIC?	☐ YES	☐ NO

How much can you achieve?

The ideas in this book will help you minimize your carbon footprint, but don't forget, it's not about trying to reduce to zero. It's still worth being greener, even if you can't be green all over. Choose the ideas that you find attractive and goals you think you can achieve. Set up a plan and reward for yourself when you achieve your target.

Carbon offsetting

You might like to try to be "carbon neutral", that is, a zero CO_2-producer. This is virtually impossible for most people, but there are many companies that offer a solution called carbon offsetting. Every time you fly or go on a long car journey, you calculate the amount of carbon your journey will generate. Then you pay a little extra money on your fare or fuel cost to a company, which invests in a green project. This might be an alternative energy scheme or a new recycling plant, and many schemes have government backing. In theory, this offsets (makes up for) the carbon emission your journey caused. Some people like the system, but others think it's just a green con.

The three Rs

One of the easiest ways to start your green career is to follow the three Rs: Reduce, Reuse, Recycle. These simple R-rules will help you make a green contribution straight away by producing less waste, and they can all fit in with your leisure time. Reducing means cutting down on waste by using less in the first place. We can also use things again instead of just throwing them away. We can also recycle, so a new product can be made out of something that has been used before. This is much easier if your home has a recycling collection by the local authority.

If there's no recycling collection in your local area, find your nearest bottle, paper, and plastic banks.

Starting points

Here are some ideas for getting into the three Rs:

Reducing	• Buy products that use less packaging. • Don't buy more clothes than you need. • Use reusable containers.
Reusing	• Redecorate shoeboxes to store pens, pencils, and drawings. • Avoid **disposable** plates, napkins, cutlery, batteries, and barbecues. • Cut, flatten, and reuse wrapping paper, envelopes, string, and ribbons.
Recycling	• Buy products made with recycled materials, such as paper and notepads. • Sort rubbish into groups for recycling: paper and cardboard, glass, metal, and plastic. • Take old shoes and clothes to your local recycling point. • Use fruit and vegetable waste to make compost (plant fertilizer).

Eco Impact

- Making one tonne of recycled paper saves an average of 17 trees. That's enough to make about 700 phone books, and saves enough energy to heat an average home for a year.
- It takes three times as much energy to make a new plastic bottle than it does to make a recycled one.
- Recycling one plastic bottle saves enough energy to power a light bulb for 6 hours.

Three more Rs...

Here are three more Rs to help your new green lifestyle:

- *Rethink*. Ask yourself if you really need or even want certain things, such as a new mobile phone. (See the flowchart on page 6.)

- *Refuse*. Say no to things you disagree with rather than just going along with them. Decide for yourself and don't be a slave to trends.

- *Renew*. Choose renewable resources when you can. Learn about and look for symbols on paper and wood that help you do this.

...and one extra R

Respect, as in "respect your environment", both globally and locally. You and your friends can take the lead by looking after your neighbourhood environment. For example, you can make sure:

- you never drop litter
- you clean up after your pet if it fouls a public place
- pick up any litter you see in your neighbourhood.

Eco-song playlist

You could make a playlist of your favourite songs with a green theme. Search for "eco-songs playlist" online and you'll find plenty of ideas. One classic on the web lists is "Big Yellow Taxi" by Joni Mitchell. It begins and ends "They paved paradise, put up a parking lot". Look through your collection and list some good eco-friendly songs to share green ideas with your friends.

Freecycle

"Changing the world one gift at a time" is the slogan of the Freecycle network, which has nearly 9 million members around the world. This successful non-profit movement is all about reuse and, as it says, "keeping good stuff out of landfills". You could use the network to give away unwanted stuff and get stuff for free from others in the same way. Visit www.freecycle.org.

Thinking big...

The way you approach a green lifestyle can combine big and small thinking. The big issue concerns the enormous environmental problems facing the planet. After all, that's why it's important for all of us to go green. Many documentaries, such as *An Inconvenient Truth* and David Attenborough's *Frozen Planet* series, have made people think about climate change for the first time. Many viewers don't find this easy, because it's such an overwhelming problem.

Imagine the polar icecaps melting, sea levels rising, and cities facing the threat of major flooding. These are the big concerns that make us think.

...and small

It's tempting to think, "Well, there's nothing I can do to stop polar ice melting, so what's the point in bothering?" But that would be missing the point. None of us can solve the enormous problems, but we all have the power to make a small difference with every green choice we make. Imagine you were cheering on a sports team. Your voice on its own might not be heard, but a whole crowd of voices can have a powerful effect.

This boat, called *Plastiki*, is made of 12,500 reclaimed plastic bottles – a big reuse and recycle campaign! In 2010, its crew sailed right across the Pacific Ocean from San Francisco to Sydney.

Don't get greenwashed!

Some companies tend to exaggerate their green credentials. The deceptive use of green claims is called **greenwashing**, and the campaign group Greenpeace is so concerned about this problem that it runs a special website (stopgreenwash.org), where you can see examples. In 2011, they claimed that several US airlines advertised that they were "flying cleaner", while at the same time the airlines' lawyers were doing their best to stop new anti-pollution programmes.

Being green - summing up

- Green means environmentally friendly.
- There are good personal and global reasons why we should all care about the environment.
- Calculate and reduce your carbon footprint.
- Reduce, reuse, recycle, rethink, refuse, renew, and respect.
- Think big (global warming) and small (every little bit helps).
- Watch out for greenwashing.

Green options at home

You probably spend most of your free time at home, so that's where the idea of eco-leisure really comes in. Perhaps you're already much greener than you think? Some of the ideas here may be so simple that you started doing them ages ago. Others may be new to you and provide inspiration on how to make your home life more environmentally friendly. Some depend on cooperation from your parents or guardians, who, after all, pay the bills. It will be up to you to convince them your suggestions are sensible.

Waking up to energy use

We all use electrical energy from the moment we get up. In the winter, your central heating probably wakes up before you. The heating system is not your responsibility, but one day it will be. Your parents will welcome any attempts you make to save money. So, if you get out of bed and feel the cold, don't run straight to the thermostat to turn it up. Put on a jumper instead! It's up to your parents to think about insulating your home properly, using an **energy-efficient** boiler, and so on. But you can help by simply saving energy. You could even do some exercises to warm yourself up on cold mornings!

There's more than one way to get some exercise at home! You can have fun burning your own energy.

fluorescent light bulb

incandescent light bulbs

Eco Impact

If you have any old-fashioned incandescent light bulbs in your house, be aware that at least 90 per cent of the energy they use is given off as heat (not light)! So, persuade your parents to buy newer fluorescent bulbs that use five times less energy and last up to twelve times longer.

Why bother to save energy?

Much of the energy we use, including electricity, comes from fossil fuels. We are using more of these fuels than ever before, and one day they will run out. These fuels also pollute the atmosphere with waste gases when they are burned to give off energy. Renewable sources of energy are much better for the environment, and some electricity companies supply power only from these. They include **biomass**, geothermal, solar, water, and wind power.

Switch off

Now, here's an obvious idea when it comes to saving energy: turn lights off when they're not being used! When you head for the bathroom, remember to switch off in the bedroom. By the way, has anyone ever told you that turning lights off (and then on again) uses more energy than leaving them on? Well, it's not true, so don't try to use that old excuse!

Bathroom routine

Do you ever leave the tap running when you brush your teeth? If so, you have an easy way to improve your green account! Turning the tap off while you brush could save up to 9,000 litres (1,980 gallons) of water a year. The same applies in the kitchen: don't let the water run more than it needs to. In regions of the world where water is always short, people would never dream of washing vegetables under running water: they use a container. It's a habit, not a chore they always have to think about. By the way, hand-washing dishes typically uses about 30 litres (6.6 gallons) of water. If the dishes are rinsed under a running tap, the total can rise to 60 litres (13.2 gallons).

One study discovered that teenagers use 95 litres (21 gallons) of water for their shower! That's almost as much water as having a bath (see below).

Shower versus bath

Most people will tell you that a shower uses less water than a bath. But of course it depends how big the bath is and how long you shower for! A medium-sized bath holds about 150 litres (33 gallons) of water, and let's say we two-thirds fill it and so use about 100 litres (22 gallons) of water per bath. The average shower uses about 10 litres (2.2 gallons) of water per minute, so if you shower for 5 minutes, you use 50 litres (11 gallons) – half the bathwater. But surveys show that people tend to take between 8 and 10 minutes over their shower, so it's all about keeping your time under the shower short.

Saving water every day

If you showered for one minute less every day, you would save about 3,650 litres (803 gallons) of water a year. You would also save the energy that would be used to heat that water. One way to cut your time down is to turn the shower off while you shampoo your hair. For one week, time yourself every day. You may have a surprise when you see how long your shower routine is! Another tip is to persuade your parents to have a flow limiter fitted to the shower. This cheap piece of equipment can reduce the flow per minute to 4–6 litres (0.9–1.3 gallons), half the normal amount, and you still get a good shower!

Day	Minutes
Mon	7
Tue	6
Wed	6 ½
Thu	6
Fri	5 (success!)
Sat	5 ½
Sun	6

Your shower timings might give you a surprise. Set yourself a 5-minute target.

Why bother to save water?

Water is a precious resource, which all living things need to live. As the world's population grows, more parts of the world are suffering from "water stress". Many **developing countries** are very short of fresh drinking water. The average Briton uses 149 litres (33 gallons) of water a day; the average American uses 575 litres (126 gallons). In poor parts of Africa, many people have to live on less than 40 litres (9 gallons) per day. The average in Mozambique is 4 litres (0.9 gallons).

Computer time

Chances are, one of the first things you look at in the morning is your computer. You will probably look at it for several hours during the day if you don't go out. A US survey from 2010 found that 8 to 18-year-olds spend more than 7½ hours surfing the internet, playing video games, or watching TV. And most are multitaskers. Forty per cent use another medium, such as a music player or a mobile phone, while on their computer. They also spend about an hour and a half texting each day.

Multitasking by using two or three devices at the same time can use up a lot of electricity.

Watch out for stand-by

Do you usually leave your computer or other appliances on? Well, that really is a waste of energy, because stand-by mode often uses 6–20 **watts** of electricity. Look at these figures for the amount of watts used by a typical laptop in different modes:

Device	Watts
fully on, charging	44.3
fully on, charged	29.5
sleep	15.8
stand-by (off)	8.9
power supply only	4.4

This band is playing in a park in San Diego, USA in celebration of International Earth Day. This special green date comes round every year on 22 April.

Laptop versus desktop

The average laptop uses up to 85 per cent less energy than a desktop computer. Even on "idle" or "sleep" mode, laptops are far more energy-efficient, using about a tenth of the power of a desktop. Here are some tips to save computer energy:

- Switch your computer off when you're not using it. Powering down could lengthen a laptop's life.
- Use the power management function on your computer (via the control panel or system preferences).
- Turn the monitor off whenever you can; it uses about two thirds of the energy needed to power the computer.
- Run your laptop off the mains rather than the battery when you can, to reduce energy lost through battery charging and discharging.
- Don't rush to upgrade to the latest computer with a faster processor; it will use more electricity.

Eco Impact

You can drive more than 3 kilometres (1.9 miles) in an electric car or make 12 mugs of tea with the energy needed to download the average album. This is still up to 80 per cent more energy-efficient than buying a CD. However, if you decide to burn a CD of your new album, this would be nearly three times as energy-wasteful as buying the album on a CD in the first place.

Online shopping

Which do you think are greener, retail shops or e-shops? According to research, an average trip to a shopping centre produces more than 4 kilograms (9 pounds) of CO_2, compared with a van-based delivery of about 180 grams (6 ounces). Per product, e-commerce warehouses use about one-sixteenth of the energy used by retail shops. However, there is a downside: goods bought online need strong packaging, which takes energy to make and creates waste.

Here are a few tips to make online shopping greener:

- Go online only for products that you can't get locally.
- Try to buy from one e-seller, saving on packaging and delivery.
- Stick to e-retailers that state they use recycled packaging.
- Use non-express postal services.
- Download music, films, and books – there's no packaging or shipping. Just make sure it's legal!

Technotrash

So, what should you do with old CDs, jewel cases, and the hardware your parents bought to play them on? You may have heard of gardeners using strings of old CDs to scare birds away. There are lots of other craft projects for which they might be useful. However, there are companies that will take this kind of gear – called technotrash or **e-waste** – and dispose of it properly or, even better, recycle it. Just search online for "recycle CDs", "recycle technotrash", or "recycle e-waste" and you'll find loads of possibilities.

This is an unusual wall hanging. How many more ways to reuse your old CDs can you think of?

20

Recycled glitter ball

Here's a good way to put your old CDs to reuse. Make a glittering decoration or disco ball!

You will need:

lots of old CDs, glue, nylon thread or string, a sphere (You could use an old plastic ball, a round paper lantern or light shade, or you could make your own papier mâché sphere as shown below.)

Method:

1. Blow up a round balloon. To make papier mâché, tear old newspaper into strips. Mix one cup of flour with two cups of water until the mixture is smooth.

2. Coat each paper strip with paste, removing any lumps with your fingers.

3. Cover the balloon with one layer of strips in one direction and a second layer in the other direction. Stick on at least four layers and leave to dry for two days.

4. Pierce a hole in the top and push a piece of knotted string into it for a hanger. Secure it with strong glue or tape.

5. Wear goggles to protect your eyes from splinters. Cut the CDs into small shapes. Make sure there are no small children around who may accidentally swallow the pieces, and take care not to cut or scratch yourself.

6. Glue the CD pieces mirror-side out all around the ball. Start from the centre and fit the shapes in as you go.

7. Hang the glitter ball up and shine a light at it to make it sparkle. If you use a ball, glue on nylon thread for hanging up before sticking on the CDs.

Your most prized possession?

In 2011, a survey of British teenagers found that three-quarters of them said their most prized possession was their mobile phone. So, it's not really surprising to discover their greatest fear was having their phone confiscated by their parents as punishment. Fifteen per cent of the teenagers questioned admitted this regularly happened to them. They also admitted the main reason for confiscation was overspending their phone budget. A US survey discovered that teenagers make or receive an average of only six mobile calls every day. However, they send or receive 96 text messages (quite a lot!). No wonder the mobile is a teenager's most prized possession!

Solar chargers

It's obvious to anyone that it's greener to use rechargeable batteries than the single-use kind. Try to use them for all your portable devices. Rechargeables are built into mobile phones, but did you know there are also solar chargers on the market, for use with your mobile, as well as your iPod or laptop? The charger builds up a store of electricity from its solar cells when left in the light. You then plug your device into the charger when you are low on power. The charger itself is small and portable, so you can take it with you on holiday or simply when you're out and about.

This solar-powered charger is being used to load up a mobile phone battery.

The world now has more than 5.6 billion mobile phones and some are greener than others.

How green is your mobile?

You may have heard horror stories about "conflict minerals", especially in Central Africa, being used in the manufacture of mobile phones. The sale of these minerals may be used to fund wars and may result in serious human rights abuses. There are campaigns you can join to protest against this problem, which seems to affect all mobile phone manufacturers. There are other issues, too, such as the use of toxic chemicals, problems of e-waste, and poor working conditions in factories.

Greenpeace International publishes an online Guide to Greener Electronics, which ranks leading mobile phone, TV, and PC manufacturers on their impact on the environment, production techniques, and attempts to make their operations more **sustainable**. The guide also gives points for energy efficiency, use of recycled plastic, and many other factors. To check out your make, go to www.greenpeace.org and search for "guide to greener electronics".

Being green – summing up

- Switch off lights and switch to fluorescent light bulbs.
- Save water in the shower.
- Reduce energy use by stopping stand-by.
- Laptops are greener than desktops.
- Online shopping is green but has disadvantages, too.
- Find ways to deal with technotrash and e-waste.
- Use a solar charger for your mobile.

Fun with friends

It's not always easy to keep up your green credentials with your friends. You may have to convince some of them that green ideas are worth pursuing. A lot of the time you spend together involves modern technology and gadgets, but there are many ways you and your friends can use modern technology in a greener way.

Conducting a survey

You spend a lot of time with your friends, and you probably all have similar problems and worries. Like you, they may be interested in trying to be greener in their leisure time. But have you ever discussed green issues together? If not, you should try it. Next time you get together, suggest you spend half an hour throwing out ideas and sharing experiences. Another way to do this would be to carry out a survey:

- Have you tried one of the new solar-powered phone chargers?

- Do you have any special ways of saving energy at home?

- Can you think of a project that we could do together to help our local community?

Since video games are interactive, you can always play them on your own. But playing with other gamers can be even more fun.

Video games

In the United States, video game systems use enough electricity to power a city the size of San Diego (bigger than Britain's second city, Birmingham). That's a great deal of energy, and according to the US National Resources Defense Council, turning off game consoles when not in use could save individuals an average of £63 a year. The Council's study found the greenest system is Nintendo Wii, which uses less power than its competitors. Here are some tips to green up your gaming:

- Turn off the console when it's not in use. Idle machines use almost as much energy as active ones.
- Activate the power-save mode. This is often buried in the menus and very difficult to find, but it's well worth the effort.
- Don't watch films on your game system. This can use five times more power than watching them on players such as Blu-Ray.

Electronic versus paper communication

Which is greener, an email or a letter? Here are some issues:

- Paper is from a renewable source (managed forests). Computers are made from non-renewable materials (oil, metals, and minerals) that have to be mined and refined.
- It takes a lot more energy to manufacture a computer than it does paper, but they are difficult to compare like for like.
- Manufacturing both causes acid rain and water pollution.
- It is much easier to recycle paper, and more people do so. E-waste, including old computers, is a big problem.

If you already own a computer then it is greener to send emails. But if you look at the bigger picture, then paper is the greener option. In any case, avoid doubling up – don't print emails.

It's eco-party time!

Next time you throw a party at home for your friends, make it a green party. Start by sending e-vites (emailed invitations) instead of buying cards, envelopes, and postage stamps. Many charities offer an e-card service, and you could consider donating the money saved to a good cause. You will be promoting the charity to your friends.

Eco-friendly food

What sort of food are you going to offer your guests? You definitely want it to be environmentally friendly, so the first thing you could think about is **organically** grown food. The word "organic" describes farming methods that do not use **pesticides** or artificial fertilizers on crops, or chemical treatments on animals. Foods that are labelled organic must come from land that has been farmed in this natural way for at least two years. **Organic farming** is definitely greener, providing healthy food and using less energy. Experts have calculated that industrial farming can mean burning 10 calories of fossil fuels to produce one calorie of food.

When you buy fruit from your local farmers' market, you know it has not travelled too far. If you're not sure, ask where the produce has come from.

Go local

If you buy your food at local shops, you can avoid building up **food miles**. This is the distance food travels from where it is grown to where it is consumed. It is estimated that in the United Kingdom, food travels 30 billion kilometres every year to feed the nation. Try to buy from local shops or farmers' markets and avoid supermarkets, which buy food from long distances away. At the same time, you'll have another green advantage: you'll be supporting members of your local community, whether you live in a big city or a small village. If we don't support our local shops, they may close. Then we'll have no choice but to give our custom to the large national and international retailers.

Waste and precycling

The best way to avoid waste is to precycle, which means pre-recycling or preventing recycling. Do this by avoiding packaging and disposable items. Here are some precycling tips:

- Take reusable bags to go shopping (see page 5).
- Buy foods with the least amount of packaging or none at all. Fruit and vegetables can be loose rather than wrapped in plastic.
- If there has to be packaging, check that it is recycled (look for the special symbol shown on the right).
- Don't buy disposable items such as paper plates or napkins.
- Avoid expanded polystyrene packaging, which is not accepted by many recyclers and is the most difficult material to break down in landfill.
- Cardboard, aluminium, steel, glass, and plastic containers can be recycled more easily.

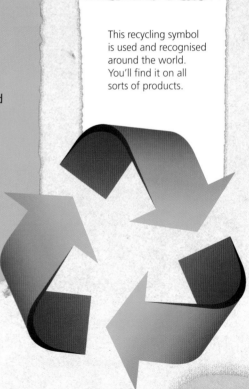

This recycling symbol is used and recognised around the world. You'll find it on all sorts of products.

Dispose of disposable dishes

At your party, use china plates, metal cutlery, and cloth napkins – even though it will mean a lot more washing-up afterwards! If your household has a dishwasher, set it on economy wash for a full load and it will use less hot water than washing up by hand.

Eating out

For your own or someone else's birthday, you and your friends might want to go out for a meal. To make sure you choose somewhere that shares your wish to be green, you'll need to do some research. You can look at the restaurant's website, if it has one. But there is no substitute for going along on foot or by bike and having a proper look at the place itself. Many food websites and magazines also list restaurants that are particularly green and serve organic food.

You can eat with your friends at a local pizzeria. If you want to check out the restaurant's green credentials, look for the points listed on the next page.

Green stars

The Green Restaurant Association was founded in San Diego, USA, in 1990. It says that it aims "to provide convenient and cost-effective tools to help the restaurant industry reduce its harmful impact on the environment". The GRA, now based in Boston, Massachusetts, USA, visits restaurants and awards stars according to scores against seven different test categories. The tests are for:

- water efficiency
- waste reduction and recycling
- sustainable furnishings and building materials
- sustainable food (from organic and local family farms)
- energy use
- use of disposables
- chemical and pollution reduction.

In the United Kingdom, The Sustainable Restaurant Association (www.thesra.org) was established in 2010 to do a similar job to GRA.

Checking out credentials

Check out the credentials of your local restaurants. A small restaurant in London was given a green award for offering these advantages:

- Up to 80 per cent of waste is recycled and the restaurant is testing new waste management strategies.
- Reusable cutlery and eco-friendly takeaway containers.
- Packaging is sent back to the supplier for reuse when possible.
- A choice of serving sizes, creating less food waste.
- Herbs grown on site.
- Open to the public, schools, and trainee chefs as an educational resource.
- Water purified on site.
- Green electricity (from renewable sources).
- All food bought from local producers.

There are lots of ways for restaurants to gain a good green rating.

Green your Halloween

You could always come up with green ideas for special parties and gatherings. Here are a few green ideas for Halloween:

- For your costume, reuse clothing you already own or visit a local charity shop for inspiration.
- If you decide to use make-up, make sure it's non-toxic.
- For sweets and treats, look for Fairtrade and/or organic chocolate.
- As well as carving faces in pumpkins, roast the seeds and use the flesh to make delicious pumpkin soup. You'll find lots of good recipes in cookbooks and online.

Outdoor activities

As well as parties and special events, there are lots of green outdoor activities you can do with your friends. At the same time you can help your local community.

You can make quite an impression with a simple old sheet!

Pedal power

If you enjoy cycling with your friends, maybe you could do more pedalling on your own, too? You could use a bike for riding to school, visiting friends, and nipping to the shops. You'll need to get a good helmet, front and rear lights, and a reflective vest. Another good green idea is the city cycle hire scheme. You can hire a bike from a special stand, such as the Barclays cycle hire, known as "Boris" bikes, in London. You pay a fee at the docking station and can drop the bike off later at another station.

Biking...

The great thing about cycling is there are no **greenhouse gases** involved. Bikes cause no pollution. They also take up very little space, so there's plenty of room on the road or on the cycle path. When you ride instead of getting a lift, you are doing your bit for the planet. You are helping yourself, too, because cycling is a great way to stay fit. It's also a good way to make new friends. But there are a few things you should think about to stay green in the saddle:

- Learn how to mend a flat tyre yourself and always expend only your own energy by using a hand pump.
- When it gets dark, use a dynamo or another rechargeable light.
- Don't bother with flashy aerodynamic cycling outfits. But safety must always come first, so wear reflective clothing.
- You don't really need sports drinks and energy bars, either; everyday organic food and drink will do. Water is the best thing you can drink to stay hydrated.

If you want to see how green your bike rides are, take the quiz on: sierraclub.org/howgreen/bikeride.

This young man from Rosario, Argentina, made his own bike frame out of bamboo, an environmentally friendly material (see page 34).

...and hiking

All kinds of hiking can also be green and can be great fun to do with friends. If you go out rambling in the countryside, there are certain rules to follow (see page 44). The most important green rule is to leave no trace of your presence. Of course, you can also have great green fun enjoying a walk in town, where the same rules apply.

Local initiatives

You could have more green fun with your friends by taking part in local initiatives. Most local authorities have a whole range of environmental projects underway at any one time. They are always looking for young volunteers to help carry out these initiatives. For some you might need the approval of your parents or another adult. Such projects are also a great way to make friends with other like-minded people. Local projects will obviously require little travel. They might involve surveys, questionnaires, or passing on information to raise awareness of environmental topics. These might cover the benefits of recycling, the problems of littering, or ways in which to improve or restore local **habitats**. You can get help, advice, and ideas from non-profit organizations such as EcoTeams (ecoteams. org.uk).

Amsterdam, Netherlands, is a cycling city. It has 600,000 bikes, many for hire, and you can ride along 400 kilometres (250 miles) of special cycle paths.

Local science survey

In 2011, two British universities asked for volunteers to help with a survey of their local horse chestnut (or conker) trees. This kind of tree is being damaged by the caterpillars of leaf-mining moths. The insects came originally from southern Europe and were first discovered in Britain in 2002. The volunteers were asked to make a survey of their local trees and report on damage. They were also encouraged to collect leaves, put them in plastic bags, and then see how many moths eventually emerged. This is the sort of project for which a group of committed teenagers is ideal. You would be helping scientists and the local community as well as learning about ecology.

On your own initiative

Do you or your friends have any ideas about local environmental issues? You might not have thought about this before, but you could begin by getting some friends together to talk about your local community. The issues you raise will vary according to your location, and whether you live in the middle of a big city or in the country. You could do some online research before meeting your friends, so that you can put forward ideas.

These pupils from a school in Michigan, USA, are planting vegetation to help stabilize a river bank. This is an excellent example of a successful local initiative.

Check out what's going on

Your local authority's website will probably list the green initiatives that are already underway in your area. This will put you in touch with existing projects. Many authorities also have a regular email newsletter that will keep you informed of work in progress. There may be an online directory, which will help you find other volunteer groups near to you. You can be sure that other groups will be pleased to hear from you, especially if you are offering help. For example, you may be planning to clean up and de-litter the banks of a local pond or stream. Other groups may have experience and could help you with planning by pointing out problems you may encounter.

33

Green sports gear

If you want to become greener in the sport you do, you can make a contribution by making sure that your equipment and clothing are as environmentally friendly as possible. For example, you can buy skateboards, snowboards, and surfboards made of bamboo or hemp. The fibres from these plants are sometimes called **eco-fibres**. Both plants are fast-growing, need no chemical pesticides, and require less water than other plants. So, they can be farmed in a more sustainable way than trees or other woody plants. Their eco-fibres can also be used for making clothing. As well as these materials, for all your outdoor sports you can wear clothes such as underwear and fleece made from recycled materials; recycled rubber-soled walking boots; and organic cotton clothes.

Make your sporting activities greener by thinking about what you wear and what you use. For some green tips on winter holidays, see page 46.

From (green) tee to green

Are you a keen golfer, or are you thinking of taking up golf? You may know that many environmentalists have criticized the game for the ecological damage they claim it causes. Critics say that golf courses take up far too much land, changing the landscape and reducing **biodiversity**. They need vast amounts of water and are often treated with fertilizers and pesticides. But things are changing, and many of the people who run golf courses are trying to reduce golf's impact on the landscape.

Surfers Against Sewage

The organization Surfers Against Sewage (SAS) runs a campaign for clean, safe surfing water free from sewage pollution, toxic waste, and plastic litter. The SAS says that scientific studies have shown that people using British beaches, lakes, and rivers for water sports are at great risk of illness caused by polluted water. "In some cases this risk is three times greater than your typical bather because sports like surfing involve more immersion and ingestion of water," they say. Members of the organization report any pollution they find to the health authorities. They also help to clean up beaches, and hold educational talks to spread the green word.

You and your friends can organize your own fun game of baseball, softball, or rounders. Or you could join a club to work on your skills more seriously.

Being green - summing up

- Survey and learn about your friends' green ideas.
- Save energy on your video games.
- Paper communication still has a lot going for it.
- Look out for eco-friendly, local food.
- Go biking and hiking, which are great green activities and a good way to make friends.
- Take part in local initiatives as a leisure activity.
- Check whether your sports are green.

Travelling green

Travelling can have an enormous environmental impact, so you should always consider how and why you go to places. For local trips, you can decide to go on foot or by bike. For longer journeys or holidays, the transport you use might not be your decision. Your parents, adult relatives, or friends may decide for you. But it's just as well to know the facts, and they might help you come up with ideas for greener family holidays.

The green way to go

Travelling by rail is usually best in terms of low carbon emissions. A coach is about the same. Car travel depends very much on the number of passengers. Four or more people can sometimes compete with travelling by diesel train over the same distance.

You can be aware of green travel and still have a great family holiday.

What about flying? Well, we all have to accept that aircraft are extremely polluting. They emit gases and particles high in the atmosphere, which is particularly damaging. They emit water vapour, which is also a greenhouse gas. It has been estimated that aircraft contribute 3 per cent of all greenhouse gases from human sources. This is set to rise to 5 per cent by 2050. Flying counts for 40 per cent of global tourism emissions. In 2008, an aviation conference predicted that total CO_2 pollution from aircraft could double by 2025. Nevertheless, we must accept that flying to a destination is sometimes the only practical or even affordable option. But we can all aim to look for alternatives when possible.

Figures for a journey

These figures show the amount of CO_2 produced by different types of transport for different numbers of passengers. There's a low and high estimate for each, calculated by Forum for the Future, a non-profit organization. The figures are higher than those sometimes quoted by transport companies, because they include emissions all the way from mining the fuel to the fuel tank in the vehicle.

The first three sets of figures assume a certain average number of total passengers in the plane, train, or bus. The car figure is worked out for the vehicle, so gets more efficient with more passengers. The figures are for a journey from London, UK, to Budapest, Hungary. This is about 1,600 kilometres (1,000 miles), roughly the same distance as New York City to Minneapolis, or Sydney to Port Augusta.

	passengers	kg carbon/ low estimate	kg carbon/ high estimate
By air	1	276	425
	2	552	850
	4	1,104	1,700
By rail	1	52	219
	2	104	438
	4	208	876
By road: coach	1	51	185
	2	102	369
	4	204	738
By road: car	1	302	608
	2	302	608
	4	302	608

One of the advantages of train travel is that you can read or use your computer in comfort.

Air travel: What do you think?

What's your opinion about air travel? This is a tricky issue, and you could discuss it with your friends when you talk about going green. Here are some questions for you to weigh up:

- Do you think governments should restrict international air travel? If so, how would they do this? Should holidaymakers be discouraged from making long journeys? What about business travellers? What about people with families who live in other countries?

- The International Air Transport Association (IATA) is the governing body that regulates air travel. It says that its aim is "to achieve carbon neutral growth in the medium term and to build a plane that produces no emissions within 50 years". Airlines have improved fuel efficiency and reduced CO_2 emissions by 14 per cent over the past 10 years. They say they have reduced fuel use and CO_2 emissions per passenger kilometre by 70 per cent compared to the 1970s. Do you think more should be done?

- Do you agree with a carbon tax on airlines? In 2012, the European Union (EU) introduced a charge on flights based on their carbon emissions. The tax applies to all airlines landing planes in EU countries, but Chinese airlines refused to pay the tax and risked fines. Do you think the tax is a good idea?

- Airlines will surely pass increased costs, such as a carbon tax, on to passengers. Maybe air travel is too cheap, anyway? Compared with other costs, air travel is much less expensive than 25 years ago. Given what we now know about the problems of global warming, is this right? What do you and your friends think? You could debate it!

Let the train take the strain

This phrase was a slogan used in advertising by British Rail. As we saw earlier, rail comes out well in the green stakes. For longer journeys, new high-speed rail schemes and undersea tunnels make trains a real alternative to planes. Also, a railway station can be in the heart of a city, while an airport is kilometres outside. Unfortunately, for long journeys rail can be more expensive than air travel, and building major new rail lines can have a huge environmental impact.

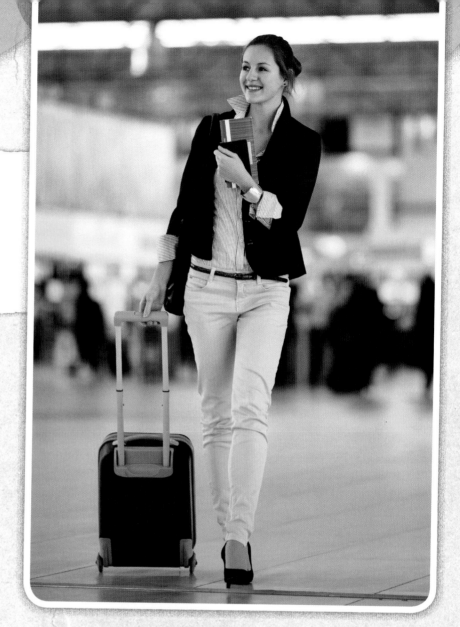

Air travel is fast and convenient. We have become very used to the option of flying. But do we rely on it too much? Is it time to rethink our attitude to planes?

Greener fuels

Greener fuels have been developed for cars and buses. These include **biofuels** (such as ethanol), electricity, and other power sources. Hybrid cars combine a petrol engine with an electric motor. At slow speeds, in town, the car runs on electricity. On faster roads, it switches to petrol and recharges the electric battery. One of the most interesting developments is hydrogen-powered fuel cells, which generate electricity to power vehicles. This is a green solution, because all that is needed are hydrogen and oxygen, with water as a harmless by-product. The problem scientists still have to solve is that it takes a lot of energy to split hydrogen from other substances.

Two-wheeled eco-carrier

Do you sometimes leave your bike at home because you have a lot of things to carry? Well, you can make your bike more useful by turning it into a kind of eco-vehicle. You could carry your load in a basket or handlebar bag at the front. The basket could be made of wicker or wire mesh, and you could use the mounting point for your front light. Or you could fit a saddlebag under your seat, with a quick-release mechanism, so that you can get the things you need in a flash.

Alternatively, you could fit a pannier or rack bag. They are best fitted in balanced pairs to a rack over your front or rear wheels. They can carry lots of stuff and come in a range of designs and fabrics, from the traditional to the high-tech and waterproof, useful in all weathers. These bike extras could go a long way to making your life greener. They also take the strain off your back so you don't have to carry a large rucksack.

Here is an excellent example of an eco-vehicle! This rider is carrying panniers on both front and back wheels, as well as using bags attached to the seat and to the handlebars.

Let's share

If you have to get a regular lift to school or anywhere else, try to make sure the car is as full as possible. A car with a driver and four passengers is much greener than four cars with one passenger each! You could talk to your parents and friends about starting up a car-sharing scheme. Adults can take it in turns to drive, and they will soon see how much time and money they save. At the same time, you will be doing your bit to save the planet a few exhaust emissions.

If your parents or other adults are interested, there are also lots of car-share schemes with dedicated websites. In some cities, there are special "car pool" lanes, so that eco-friendly car-sharers have an easier, faster journey.

Going public

Using buses, trams, and trains helps reduce the volume of traffic on the roads, reducing congestion and helping you limit your carbon footprint. If there are twenty people on the bus, it's the same as five of the shared cars we mentioned. Many towns and cities now have integrated systems, so you can travel on buses, trams, underground and overland trains on one ticket. Encourage your car-bound friends to join you on public transport.

Being green - summing up

- Travel on foot or by bike whenever you can.
- Compare different methods of transport for eco-friendliness.
- Travel by rail, bus, coach, or tram for longer journeys.
- Should we think about putting more carbon tax on aircraft?
- Greener fuels and hybrid cars will help.
- Turn your bike into an eco-vehicle by adding accessories.
- Encourage adults to share cars and journeys.
- Use public transport.

Eco-holidays

The International Ecotourism Society defines ecotourism as "responsible travel to natural areas that conserves the environment and improves the well-being of local people". Environmentalists are very concerned that tourists should travel responsibly because, however hard they try, it's difficult for them not to leave their mark on their destination. When we are tourists, we all inevitably create waste and pollution. The problem is growing all the time. In 1970, there were about 175 million international tourists. By 2010, this number had grown to more than 940 million.

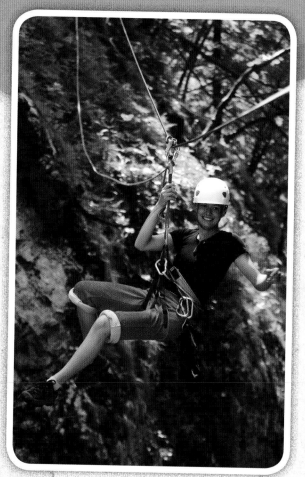

Responsible tourism ensures that extreme sports and other activities do not harm the environment.

Responsible tourism

When we go on holiday, we all want to be responsible. What does that actually mean? Will it help us to be green, too? At a conference in Cape Town, South Africa, representatives from all over the world drew up guidelines in a declaration. They said that responsible tourism:

- needs to minimise negative environmental and social impacts
- generates greater economic benefits for local people
- involves local people in decisions that affect their lives
- makes positive contributions to **conservation**
- provides understanding of local cultural and social issues
- provides access for physically challenged people
- engenders respect between tourists and local people.

Staying in a green hotel

If your family plans to stay in a hotel, there are ways you can make it a greener holiday. The US Green Hotel Initiative helps travellers ask for environmentally friendly services when they check in. For example, a Guest Request Card asks the hotel to replace toiletries only when they are used up. You could take cards like this (available from www.ceres.org), or make your own list, whatever you choose, it's best to speak to staff at the hotel when you arrive.

In theory, the hotel owners should be pleased, because you are asking for things that will save them money. Some hotels have their own cards. You could make your own list with your parents or the adults you are travelling with. What points would you like to make?

☐ Do not replace sheets and towels every day

☐ Keep the air conditioning turned down

☐ Recycle plastic bottles and paper

Saving on resources

When you're away, you can save on resources just as you do at home. In your hotel, or wherever else you're staying, try to make sure you:

- turn off lights and other electrics when you leave
- don't waste water
- use only the toiletries you need
- reuse towels, bathrobes, and sheets until they need washing
- keep the rest of your laundry to a minimum.

Can you add some other points?

An eco-festival or eco-fair is a great destination for a day out. You can have fun and pick up some green ideas at the same time.

Off to the green countryside

We all know that trips to the countryside, including rambling and camping, are great fun. We also know there have to be special green rules so that the countryside stays green for us and others to enjoy. Imagine standing at a beautiful spot to admire the view and seeing out of the corner of your eye a cigarette butt, sweet wrapper, or piece of toilet paper. View ruined!

Here are some basic tips to follow in the countryside:
- Leave no trace, so that you have a natural habitat to return to. With a little planning, it's easier than you think. Take rubbish bags so that you don't leave any waste.
- Never leave even the smallest piece of litter. Stuff wrappers in your pockets or backpack.
- Stay on paths. Every time you stray off a path, you create an opening for others to follow, which will eventually widen the trampled area.
- Use unbreakable dishes and utensils rather than disposable paper or polystyrene versions.
- Wash dishes and yourself with non-toxic, **biodegradable** soap.
- Shower and wash dishes using as little water as possible.
- Dump grey water (old dishwater) in designated areas, away from fresh water sources, and not in the bushes.

The Countryside Code

The English Countryside Code is a list of five common-sense general rules to help everybody respect, protect, and enjoy the countryside.
- Be safe – plan ahead and follow any signs.
- Leave gates and property as you find them.
- Protect plants and animals and take your litter home.
- Keep dogs under close control.
- Consider other people.

When nature calls

This is a tricky topic, but a very important one. Human waste is unsightly and can present a health hazard, so we must all deal with human biology. Experienced green ramblers and campers use plastic or metal containers that travel in empty and out full.

Casual ramblers should follow these guidelines:
- Look out for toilets along the way and use them when you can.
- Find a private spot far away from water sources – at least 50 metres (164 feet) from a river, stream, or lake.
- Dig a hole at least 15 centimetres (6 inches) deep; a trowel is useful for this.
- Take toilet paper back out with you in a rubbish bag; or bury it in the hole; or burn it if it is safe to do so.
- Fill the hole back in.
- Take sanitary products with you in a rubbish bag or burn them, if it is safe to do so.

Can wildlife tourism be green?

Wildlife tourism is an important industry in many countries. It can be green so long as tourists follow the rules. Some tour companies specialize in wildlife holidays, and they will make sure you enjoy yourself and leave the animals and their habitats as you found them. In 2011, a safari tour operator based in Malawi and Zambia was joint overall winner of the Responsible Tourism Award for its excellent work with local African communities. The company runs safari camps in a Zambian National Park that is home to many species of birds and animals.

Watching wild animals in their natural habitat makes for an exciting holiday. Try to find eco options whenever you can.

Winter holidays

One of the likely results of global warming is that high-mountain areas will have less snow and ice. Winter holidays are big business and very popular, however, so many resorts in the world's skiing regions have increased their facilities to make snow and blow it on to the slopes. This uses a lot of energy. Some resorts are greener than others, so if your family is considering a winter-sports holiday, you could research your resort.

Green skiing resorts

- The resort of Lech, in the Austrian Alps, heats about nine-tenths of its ski chalets and hotels from a biomass plant that runs on wood chips and waste. It sends hot water throughout the village. This has replaced individual oil-burning boilers and got rid of the air pollution that was spoiling the town.

- The Rockies resort of Vail, Colorado, is using its 300 days of sunshine a year to increase its use of solar panels to generate energy. Vail also claims to have the largest ski-area recycling programme in the world, recycling or reusing more than 70 per cent of material on the mountain.

There are many kilometres of cross-country tracks near the Austrian mountain village of Lech. This form of skiing is becoming more popular as downhill slopes become overcrowded.

Cross-country as well as downhill

Downhill skiing and snowboarding are exhilarating and fun. That's why these sports are so popular. However, the huge numbers of downhillers are putting great strain on mountain habitats, causing erosion and other problems. One way to change this is for more of us to start skiing cross-country rather than downhill. You'll need special skis, which could be made of the sustainable timber paulownia. It's tough exercise, because you spend most of your time pushing yourself along flat snow, but it is great fun. Snowboarders or non-skiers could consider snowshoeing instead. This form of winter walking is becoming more popular.

Being green - summing up

- The tourist industry is growing all the time.
- Responsible tourism and ecotourism are green alternatives to traditional tourism.
- Ask hotels for an environmentally friendly service.
- Obey some basic rules in the countryside, when rambling or camping.
- Wildlife tourism can be green.
- Look out for greener winter holidays.
- Try cross-country skiing or snowshoeing.

Summing up: it's your choice!

There are lots of ways in which we can make our leisure time greener. We can all use energy more wisely and efficiently. We can use less water and recycle waste. We can also travel more sensibly, especially by cycling or walking whenever possible. In this book, we have looked at lots of green ideas and practical tips. You may want to take some up and you may think that some are over the top. But whatever you think, there's no denying that if every one of us tries to be just a little greener, our small actions could add up to big results. It's up to you to help. It's your choice!

The butterfly effect

In 1972, the US scientist Edward Lorenz wrote a paper that asked the question: "Does the flap of a butterfly's wings in Brazil set off a tornado in Texas?" Lorenz was referring to the weather, and his words suggested that a small action in one place can result in big changes somewhere else. We can use this as positive thinking for our small green changes. If millions of people do the same small thing, they can make a real difference.

Replacing the bottle

You could do a small thing with a big effect by giving up bottled water, especially in plastic bottles. In 2011, it was estimated that 174 billion litres (38 billion gallons) of bottled water was sold throughout the world. It takes 162 grams (8 ounces) of oil and 7 litres (12 pints) of water (including power-plant cooling water) to manufacture a 1-litre (1.7-pint) bottle. Experts have calculated that in the United States the amount of oil needed to make plastic water bottles every year is enough to fuel 100,000 cars for that same period.

Yet, in the United States bottled water generally costs about 1,000 times more than tap water. Many people believe the bottled variety is better for them, but health experts say that tap water is just as good.

If you don't like the taste of tap water, a filter system at home will make a real difference. Then all you need is a reusable stainless steel bottle to fill up before you leave the house.

Job done?

Your efforts at eco-leisure are worthwhile. But the job is never done, because there are always ways in which we can help our planet more. Think positively and celebrate your achievements. One way to do this is to keep a diary of your green decisions and actions. That way you'll be able to look back later and see what you have achieved: quite a lot! You might even decide to give yourself a small reward to celebrate success. Just make sure it's a green gift!

Quiz

The first 12 questions can be answered by reading this book. The rest may need more research! See page 55 for the answers.

1. **How much bottled water is sold around the world in a year?**
   a) 174 million litres
   b) 174 billion litres
   c) 174 thousand litres
   d) 174 litres

2. **Which effect stops heat escaping from Earth?**
   a) The hothouse effect
   b) The Greenpeace effect
   c) The greenhouse effect
   d) The atmospheric effect

3. **What does CO_2 stand for?**
   a) carbon dioxide
   b) copper dioxide
   c) carbon monoxide
   d) carbon

4. **Which is not a fossil fuel?**
   a) oil
   b) gas
   c) coal
   d) wood

5. **Which of these countries' people have the biggest average carbon footprint?**
   a) United Kingdom
   b) Canada
   c) Australia
   d) United States

6. **Which is not one of the three green Rs?**
   a) reuse
   b) rebel
   c) recycle
   d) reduce

7. **Making one tonne of recycled paper saves how many trees?**
   a) 1
   b) 7
   c) 13
   d) 17

8. **Which boat was made from reclaimed plastic bottles?**

   a) *Plastiki*   c) *Reclastiki*

   b) *Kontiki*   d) *Titaniki*

9. **How much energy does a fluorescent light bulb use compared to an incandescent bulb?**

   a) half   c) one-fifth

   b) one-third   d) none

10. **What are surfers in the SAS against?**

    a) spray   c) sea salt

    b) splashing   d) sewage

11. **What do hybrid cars combine with a petrol engine?**

    a) diesel motor   c) oil motor

    b) electric motor d) petrol tank

12. **What is a pannier?**

    a) one of a pair of bags   c) all-round view

    b) small drinking cup   d) set of musical pipes

13. **What percentage of global electricity is produced from renewable sources?**

    a) 50 per cent   c) 10 per cent

    b) 5 per cent   d) 20 per cent

14. **How many metal cans can be recycled with the energy needed to make one new one?**

    a) 20   c) 10

    b) 15   d) 5

15. **What does the recycling number 2 on plastic bottles mean?**

    a) it can be used twice   c) nothing

    b) it's made of high-density polyethylene   d) it can't be recycled

16. **Which country produces the most hydroelectricity?**

    a) China   c) Canada

    b) Brazil   d) United States

Glossary

biodegradable able to be broken down naturally by living organisms

biodiversity variety of plants and animals in a particular habitat or the world

biofuel produced from biomass, such as ethanol from sugar cane

biomass organic matter that can be used as a source of energy

carbon footprint measure of the impact you have on the planet, related to the amount of greenhouse gases produced in your daily life through burning fossil fuels for energy

climate change rising temperatures worldwide, caused by the increase of greenhouse gases in the atmosphere that trap the Sun's heat

conservation protecting wild habitats and their plants and animals

degrade to be broken down naturally by living organisms

developing country poor country that is trying to become more advanced economically

disposable made to be thrown away after being used once

eco-fibre materials from fast-growing plants, such as bamboo and hemp, that need no chemical pesticides and relatively little water

emission waste gas produced and given off

energy-efficient using as little energy as possible for a task

e-waste also known as technotrash. Electronic waste including old hardware and software, such as CDs, old mobile phones, and computers.

food miles distance that food travels from the point of origin to your table

fossil fuel energy source such as coal, gas, and oil which was formed over millions of years from the remains of animals or plants

greenhouse gas one of a group of gases, including carbon dioxide and methane, that contribute to global warming

greenwashing making a misleading claim about the environmental benefits of a product or service

habitat natural home or environment of an animal or plant

landfill area of land where large amounts of waste material are buried under the earth

organic produced without using man-made chemicals

organic farming method of farming which minimizes the use of harmful chemical fertilizers and pesticides. Organic farming is also known as all-natural farming.

pesticide chemical used to kill insects or other organisms that are harmful to crops

renewable source of energy that does not run out

sustainable way of doing something that does not use up too many natural resources or pollute the environment

watt unit of power that measures the rate of using electricity

How much energy per Google search?

Research by a Harvard University scientist shows that performing two Google searches produces the equivalent carbon dioxide of boiling a kettle (15 grams [0.5 oz] of CO_2). This figure includes all energy consumption, including that of your computer, the servers hosting the page you are looking at, and the transport of the data to your machine.

However, Google disagrees and says their servers produce only 0.2 grams (0.007 oz) of CO_2 per search. That makes a boiling kettle the same as 750 searches. They say that the following activities amount to the number of Google searches quoted:

Activity	Google searches
Recycled daily newspaper decomposing	850
Producing a glass of orange juice	1,050
Washing a load of dishes in an energy-efficient dishwasher	5,100
An 8-kilometre trip in an average car	10,000
Producing a cheeseburger	15,000

Find out more

Further reading

Generation Green: The Ultimate Teen Guide to Living an Eco-Friendly Life,
   Linda and Tosh Sivertsen (Simon Pulse, 2008)

Going Green: The Essential Guide, Cora Lydon (Need2Know, 2010)

*How to Go Carbon Neutral: A Practical Guide to Treading More Lightly Upon
   the Earth*, Mark Brassington (How To Books, 2007)

The Eco-Living Handbook: A Complete Green Guide for Your Home and Life,
   Sarah Callard and Diane Millis (Sevenoaks, 2010)

The Rough Guide to Green Living, Duncan Clark (Rough Guides, 2009)

Websites

ecoteams.org.uk
EcoTeams, linked to the environmental charity Global Action Plan,
helps people make greener choices.

foei.org
Friends of the Earth International campaigns on environmental and
social issues.

www.greenpeace.org.uk
Greenpeace is a global organization that campaigns to protect the
environment.

www.guardian.co.uk/environment/series/ask-leo-lucy
Find lots of green questions answered in a no-nonsense way and
grouped under the headings energy, fashion and clothing, food,
homes, technology, transport, and waste.

DVDs

An Inconvenient Truth, director Davis Guggenheim (Paramount, 2006)
  This Oscar-winning documentary focused on Al Gore's campaign
  to make the issue of global warming a recognized problem.

Waste Land, director Lucy Walker (Entertainment One, 2011)
  This Oscar-nominated documentary is about turning landfill
  waste into art.

More topics to research

There are many different topics related to green options and leisure.
Here are some more research ideas:

- Share your stuff: Stuff Your Rucksack is "an online community
  that helps responsible travellers make a practical difference to
  the lives of deserving people in developing countries". Travellers
  can look up charities in the places they intend to visit, as well as
  taking simple things with them that will mean a lot to those who
  receive them. Visit www.stuffyourrucksack.com.

- Water footprint: A product's water footprint is the volume of fresh
  water used to produce it. This includes the water used in all steps
  of the production chain. You could investigate this, starting with
  food. Visit www.waterfootprint.org.

- City transport: You could investigate the latest transport schemes
  around the world. Then you could compare them to where you
  live (or your nearest city). You could start by looking at the
  German "Mo'" project: visit mo-bility.com.

Answers to quiz (pages 50–51):
1 b; 2 c; 3 a; 4 d; 5 c; 6 b; 7 d; 8 a; 9 c; 10 d; 11 b; 12 a; 13 d; 14 a;
15 c; 16 b.

Index

air travel 36, 37, 38, 39

biodiversity 34
biofuels 39
biomass 15, 46
bottled water 48

camping and hiking 31, 44–45
car travel 36, 37, 39, 41
car-share schemes 41
carbon emissions 7, 8, 9, 20, 36, 37, 38, 53
carbon footprint 8–9
carbon offsetting 9
carbon tax 38
CDs 19, 20–21
climate change 7, 12
clothing 10, 30, 34
coach travel 36, 37
computer energy 18–19, 25, 53
conflict minerals 23
countryside, visiting 44–45
cycle hire 30, 32
cycling 30–31, 32, 40

dish washing 16, 28, 44
disposable items 10, 27, 44
downloading music, films, and books 19, 20

e-commerce 20
e-vites 26
e-waste (technotrash) 20, 23, 25
eating out 28–29
eco-fibres 34
eco-song playlists 11
ecology 32
ecotourism 42–43
emails 25, 26
energy saving 7, 14–15, 18–19, 25

flow limiters 17
food 26–27, 28–29, 30, 31
food miles 27

fossil fuels 8, 15, 26
Freecycle 12
friends, fun with 24–35

game consoles 25
glitter ball 21
global warming 7, 38, 46
golf 34
greenhouse gases 7, 31, 36, 47
Greenpeace 4, 13, 23
greenwashing 13

Halloween 30
heating 14
holidays 42–47
hotels 43
hybrid cars 39
hydrogen-powered fuel cells 39

International Earth Day 19

landfill 5, 12, 27
laptops 18, 19, 22
light bulbs 11, 15
litter 35, 44
local environmental initiatives 32–33

methane 5, 7
mobile phones 22–23
money saving 7

organic food 26, 28, 31
outdoor activities 30–31, 34–35, 44–47

packaging 10, 20, 27, 29
paper 5, 11, 25
parties 26–30
pesticides 26, 34
plastic bags 5
plastic bottles 11, 13, 48
pollution 5, 15, 25, 35, 36, 46
precycling 27
public transport 8, 41

rail travel 36, 37, 38, 41
reasons to be green 4, 6–7
rechargeable batteries 22
recycling 5, 9, 10, 11, 13, 27, 29, 46
recycling symbol 27
reducing 10
renewable resources 5, 11, 15, 25, 29, 46
respect for the environment 11
restaurants 28–29
reusing 5, 10, 12, 13, 29, 30, 46

seven Rs 10–11
shopping 6, 20, 26–27
showers 16–17, 44
skiing and snowboarding 46–47
solar chargers 22
sports 34–35
stand-by mode 18
switching lights off 15

tap water 48, 49
transport 8, 13
travel 30–31, 36–41

video games 25
volunteering 32, 33

warm, keeping 14
waste, human 45
waste, reducing 10, 20, 27, 29
water filters 49
water saving 16–17
water sports 35
wildlife tourism 45
winter-sports holidays 46–47